Clara Barton

A Photo-Illustrated Biography

by Kathleen W. Deady

Consultant:
Lyde Cullen Sizer
Associate Professor of U.S. History
Sarah Lawrence College
Bronxville, New York

Bridgestone Books
an imprint of Capstone Press
Mankato, Minnesota

Bridgestone Books are published by Capstone Press
151 Good Counsel Drive, P.O. Box 669, Mankato, Minnesota 56002
http://www.capstone-press.com

Library of Congress Cataloging-in-Publication Data
Deady, Kathleen W.
    Clara Barton / by Kathleen W. Deady.
    p. cm.—(A photo-illustrated biography)
    Summary: An introduction to the life of the nurse who served on the battlefields of the
Civil War and later founded the American Red Cross.
    Includes bibliographical references and index.
    ISBN 0-7368-1604-6 (hardcover)
    1. Barton, Clara, 1821–1912—Juvenile literature. [1. Barton, Clara, 1821–1912. 2. Red
Cross—United States—Biography—Juvenile literature. 3. Nurses—United States—
Biography—Juvenile literature. 4. Nurses. 5. Women—Biography.] I. Title. II. Photo-
illustrated biographies.
HV569.B3 D38 2003
361.7'634'092—dc21   2002008976

Editorial Credits
Erika Shores, editor; Karen Risch, product planning editor; Linda Clavel, cover designer
    and interior illustrator; Alta Schaffer, photo researcher

Photo Credits
Clara Barton National Historic Site, National Park Service, cover, 6, 16
Corbis, 4, 12; Lee Snider, 8
Corbis/Bettmann, 10, 14, 18, 20

1 2 3 4 5 6 08 07 06 05 04 03

Table of Contents

Clara Barton

Clara Barton was a teacher, nurse, and writer. As a humanitarian, she helped others. Clara spent her life helping people who were sick or wounded. She tried to make their lives better.

Clara started the American Red Cross. The Red Cross helps sick and wounded soldiers during wartime. It also helps victims of fire, floods, and other disasters. Clara served as president of the Red Cross from 1881 to 1904.

Clara worked hard for her beliefs. She spent her life caring for others and saved many lives. Her work encouraged millions of people to volunteer.

Clara received awards and honors for her work. Many countries recognized her brave and generous actions. People remember Clara as one of the great women in U.S. history.

Clara started the American Red Cross in 1881.

"…naturally my book education became their first care, and under these conditions it is little to say, that I have no knowledge of ever learning to read, or of a time that I did not do my own story reading."
–Clara, in her book, *The Story of My Childhood*, 1907

Early Years

Clarissa Harlowe Barton was born on December 25, 1821, in North Oxford, Massachusetts. She was the youngest of five children. Her family called her Clara.

Clara's father was Stephen Barton. He was a farmer, horse breeder, and politician. Stephen had been a soldier. He told Clara stories of the army. His stories gave her a lifelong interest in the military.

Sarah Stone Barton was Clara's mother. She cared for the home. Sarah was an independent thinker. She believed women should have the same rights as men.

Clara's brothers and sisters taught her math, spelling, and reading when she was very young. Four-year-old Clara could already spell long words when she started school. Clara was an excellent but shy student.

This photograph shows the house where Clara was born in North Oxford, Massachusetts.

> "I realize now how carefully...the whole family watched the little nurse, but I had no idea of it then. I thought my position the most natural thing in the whole world; I almost forgot that there was an outside to the house."
> –Clara, in her book, *The Story of My Childhood*, 1907

Nurse and Teacher

Even as a child, Clara helped others. When she was 11, her brother David was hurt badly when he fell from a barn roof. Clara cared for him for two years. Clara helped other children with their schoolwork. She took care of poor families when they were sick.

At age 17, Clara became a teacher. At that time, people did not need special training to teach. Clara's family thought teaching would make her less shy.

In 1850, Clara went back to school. She attended the Liberal Institute in Clinton, New York. She studied writing and languages there.

Clara taught in New Jersey the next year. In 1852, she helped open a school in Bordentown. Clara helped the school grow to more than 600 students. The school needed a principal. Clara believed she deserved the job. Officials gave the job to a man instead of to Clara. She was upset when she was not chosen for the job.

Clara opened this school in Bordentown, New Jersey. It was the town's first free public school.

"If I can't be a soldier, I'll help soldiers. When there is no longer a soldier's arm to raise the stars and stripes above our capitol, may God give strength to mine."
–Clara, in a speech, 1861

Civil War Nurse

By 1854, Clara had moved to Washington, D.C. She worked in the U.S. Patent Office. This office protects people's inventions so others cannot copy them.

In 1861, the Civil War (1861–1865) began. Clara saw wounded soldiers. She learned of the lack of supplies. Clara quit her job to help the soldiers.

Clara helped wherever she was needed. She gave speeches and asked people to donate items such as handkerchiefs, jelly, and paper for writing letters. She set up centers where people could bring their donations. She brought supplies and medicine to wounded soldiers.

Nurses were needed during the Civil War. Clara went onto many battlefields. Clara helped the doctors. She sewed up wounds. She gave food and medicine to injured soldiers. The soldiers called her the "Angel of the Battlefield."

Civil War hospitals such as the one shown in this photograph needed many nurses to care for the soldiers.

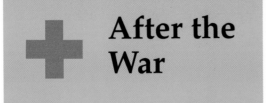

After the War

The Civil War ended in 1865. Clara continued to help the men who had served in the war. She gave food and clothing to returning soldiers. They told her about missing soldiers.

With this information, Clara made lists of soldiers who were missing and dead. She helped families locate missing soldiers by posting the soldiers' names in public places. She formed the Office of Correspondence to search for missing soldiers. In all, Clara identified 22,000 dead soldiers.

Clara raised money to support the Office of Correspondence. She gave speeches about her war experiences. Many people gave money to support the Office of Correspondence.

By August 1869, Clara was very tired. Her doctor ordered her to rest. She decided to go to Europe with her sister.

Clara formed the Office of Correspondence to find missing soldiers.

Helping in Europe

In Europe, Clara did not rest for long. She learned of the Treaty of Geneva. Many countries had signed this new agreement. It promised fair treatment to all soldiers of war. The United States had not yet signed the treaty.

Clara also learned of the International Red Cross. The Red Cross helped soldiers during war. Clara wanted to help the International Red Cross.

In Germany and France, Clara worked hard with the Red Cross. She started new hospitals. She brought supplies to soldiers. Germany gave Clara the Iron Cross for outstanding military service. She was the first woman to receive this award.

In 1873, Clara returned to the United States. She wanted the United States to agree to the Treaty of Geneva. She also hoped to start the Red Cross in the United States.

Clara joined the Red Cross in Europe. She took care of soldiers and helped start new hospitals.

American Red Cross

Clara began planning when she returned to the United States. Clara wanted a national American Red Cross with smaller offices in cities and towns across the country. She believed the Red Cross could do more than help soldiers. Clara wanted the Red Cross to help victims of fires, floods, tornadoes, and droughts.

Clara wrote articles and gave speeches about the Red Cross. In March 1881, President James Garfield took office. Clara approached him with the idea of starting an American Red Cross. Garfield thought the Red Cross was a very good idea.

On May 21, 1881, Clara held the first official meeting of the American Red Cross. Clara became its first president. In March 1882, the United States finally supported the Treaty of Geneva.

In 1897, Clara's home in Glen Echo, Maryland, became the headquarters of the American Red Cross.

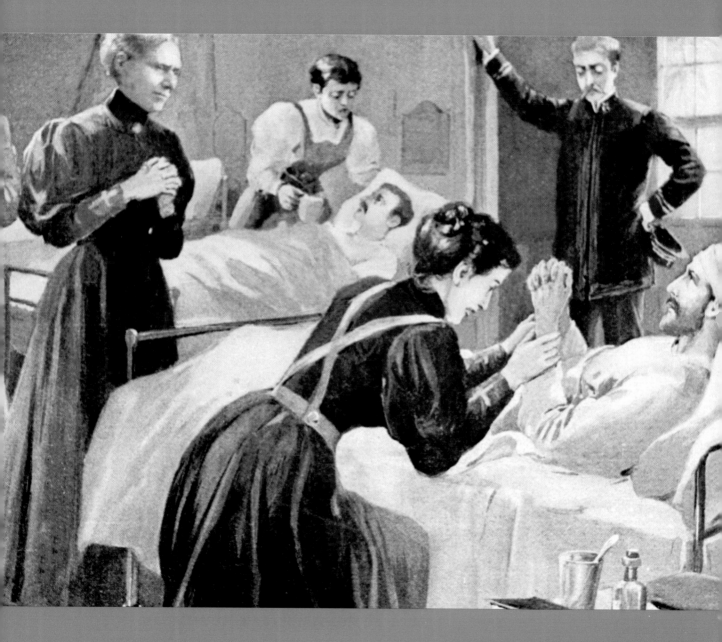

Working for the Red Cross

Clara traveled to many places to direct Red Cross workers. In 1882, she went to Michigan to help fire victims. She also went to South Carolina after an earthquake. In 1884, she traveled along the Ohio River. She took supplies to people affected by flooding along the river. In 1886, she brought food to people starving in Texas.

The work Clara did for the Red Cross took her wherever she was needed. She went to Russia in 1891 and Armenia in 1898 to help victims of natural disasters. In 1900, 79-year-old Clara spent six weeks helping flood victims in Galveston, Texas. During these years, she also wrote books about the Red Cross.

Clara (left) is shown here watching over Red Cross nurses caring for wounded soldiers in Havana, Cuba.

Later Years

Clara was 83 years old when she retired from the Red Cross on June 16, 1904. She spent the rest of her life in Glen Echo, Maryland. She was healthy and stayed active. In 1907, Clara wrote *The Story of My Childhood*.

Clara died on April 12, 1912. She was 90 years old. Clara was buried in Oxford, Massachusetts.

Clara received many honors and awards during her life. In 1890, a monument was built for her in Antietam, Maryland. The Civil War Battle of Antietam was fought on September 17, 1862. More than 23,000 men died in that battle. The monument honors the "Angel of the Battlefield" for her work that day.

Today, people remember Clara Barton as a woman of great strength and courage. She dedicated herself to helping others. Her work continues to help people around the world.

Clara served as the president of the American Red Cross for 23 years.

Fast Facts about Clara Barton

✚ After the Civil War, Clara gave more than 200 speeches about her experiences.

✚ Clara believed in equal rights for women. In 1892, Clara wrote the now famous poem, "The Women Who Went to the Field."

✚ Clara's home in Glen Echo, Maryland, was the headquarters for the Red Cross from 1897 to 1904.

Dates in Clara Barton's Life

1821—Clara is born on December 25 in North Oxford, Massachusetts.

1839—Clara begins teaching at age 17.

1850—Clara studies at the Liberal Institute in Clinton, New York.

1852—Clara helps to open a free school in Bordentown, New Jersey.

1854—Clara moves to Washington, D.C., to work in the U.S. Patent Office.

1861—The Civil War begins. Clara quits her job to help in the war effort.

1865—The Civil War ends. Clara looks for missing soldiers.

1869—Clara travels to Europe. She learns about the Treaty of Geneva and the International Red Cross.

1873—Clara returns to the United States. She works to form the American Red Cross. She also works to get the United States to agree to Treaty of Geneva.

1881—Clara holds the first official meeting of the American Red Cross.

1904—Clara retires as president of American Red Cross after 23 years.

1912—Clara dies in Glen Echo, Maryland, on April 12, 1912, at age 90.

Words to Know

humanitarian (hyoo-MAN-uh-TAIR-ee-uhn)—someone who cares about the needs of other people

independent (in-di-PEN-duhnt)—having the quality of someone who does not need or want much help from other people

monument (MON-yuh-muhnt)—a structure that is built to help people remember someone or something

patent (PAT-ent)—a document that protects people's inventions so others cannot steal the ideas

politician (pol-uh-TISH-uhn)—someone who runs for or holds a government office

treaty (TREE-tee)—an agreement between two or more nations

victim (VIK-tuhm)—a person who is hurt, killed, or made to suffer because of an accident or natural disaster

volunteer (vol-uhn-TIHR)—to give help or perform services without being asked or paid money

Read More

Francis, Dorothy Brenner. *Clara Barton: Founder of the American Red Cross.* A Gateway Biography. Brookfield, Conn.: Millbrook Press, 2002.

Mara, Wil. *Clara Barton.* Rookie Biographies. New York: Children's Press, 2002.

Ruffin, Frances E. *Clara Barton.* American Legends. New York: PowerKids Press, 2002.

Wheeler, Jill C. *Clara Barton.* Breaking Barriers. Minneapolis: Abdo, 2002.

Useful Addresses

American Red Cross Museum
Red Cross Square
1730 E Street, NW
Washington, DC 20006

**American Red Cross
  National Headquarters**
430 17th Street, NW
Washington, DC 20006-5307

Internet Sites

Track down many sites about Clara Barton.
Visit the FACT HOUND at http://www.facthound.com

IT IS EASY! IT IS FUN!

1) Go to *http://www.facthound.com*
2) Type in: 0736816046
3) Click on "FETCH IT" and FACT HOUND will
   find several links hand-picked by our editors.

Relax and let our pal FACT HOUND do the research for you!

Index